THE COLD CALL KING

BY JON ROBERT QUINN

Notes

The Cold Call King

Humble Beginnings

Selling Cars

The Pursuit

Finding Leads

Your Contacts

Getting Started

Making Calls

Referrals

Rebuttals

Understanding Marketing

The Entrepreneur's Why

Training Your Sales People (Extended Version)

Expect Good Things (Extended Version)

In Conclusion

The Cold Call King

So, you're ready to start your first business. Maybe, you've owned a business in the past. What if you already own a business? Wherever your journey is taking you as an entrepreneur, you're going to need to drum up business at one point and as boring as it sounds, cold calling is the most effective and efficient source of marketing, believe it or not.

As I sit here and write this book, I am on my eleventh-floor balcony, looking out over the California Capitol building lit up in the night sky. It's a mild seventy degrees at 11:17 pm on an August evening. My grand piano sitting to my right maybe ten feet away next to one of my many guitars I use while on tour for my music career and about three blocks from where I am sitting, at eye-level are four million-dollar condominiums that were just build maybe three months ago. I am not bragging but painting a picture of where my life is today, and without cold calls, I may be still selling cars for a few grand per month hoping and praying that someday, maybe somebody my luck would strike me rich. This is how many people think. They just hope that things will happen in their favor and with little action brings little result and most of those people find themselves disappointed.

I used to work at a mortgage company. I would make cold calls all day, every day and though I was bored out of my mind, I was very good at it. I had closed me retail stores about a year prior and the only real work experience I had since my business was when I worked at Taco Bell for a few months until I got hired to sell cars for Dodge. The mortgage company hired me for an entry-level position calling lead lists to talk about the Home Affordable Refinance Program. The atmosphere was a lot like the movie Wolf of Wall Street. People would snort coke in the bathroom. Footballs covered in one hundred-dollar bills were being thrown across the room for whoever to catch.

Sitting there for maybe ten hours a day making cold calls and being hung up on Christmas Eve was an eye opener for me. I would get to work before the sun came up and leave after the sun went down. I was working hard but wasn't working smart. I was using my back. My sales were great according to the company's expectations, but my life was so unfulfilled. I knew I was better than the rest of the sales people I worked with and once made the mistake of speaking my mind to a boss telling him that I was the smartest guy in the room. They didn't fancy that so much. Either way, I was number one in sales for the whole company for about six hundred employees. The halls were lined with record holders and record breakers and even though I was only there a year and half, it took three years for somebody to come along and break the records I set.

Well, one day I was sitting there frustrated over the fact that I was calling the same people over and over and after one sale ended, I was back to looking for the next. From there, I would set my expectations higher, exceed the company's expectations and again, make the leaderboard, looking like a hero at the end of the month. As soon as the new month started, I was back to zero and had to do it all again. There had to be a better way. Before long, I was being promoted and even in that position, exceeded expectations. Then, one day I was called into the Executive Vice President's office and it sounded like this, "Bobby, we are going to create a position for you giving you access to every Loan Officer's queue. We want every dead deal brought to life. We want fifteen deals per month to make your bonus." The first month I hit nineteen. The second month, thirty-one. They then made me an ultimatum. I get licensed and become a Loan Officer or they will have to let me go. I had become too expensive for them to keep at my current position and they wanted loans out of me. This would require me to work for one hundred percent commission and working pretty much all hours of the day. Shortly after, I left the company.

Today, many years later, I still make cold calls every single day. However, since I now run my own business, I am able to call the shots, do it my way and make as much or as little money as I want. Some days, I just want to sit by the pool or take a drive up to Lake Tahoe and shut my phone off. Let's just say that I am now one of the most popular talk show hosts in

Northern, California being voted number one FM Radio only ten months after launching my first show, The Good Life Show with Jon Robert Quinn. And all those folks at my previous job, they are all still sitting there making the same calls, the same way, making the same money and doing the same thing over and over and over again.

So, maybe I was onto something by saying I was in the smartest guy in the room. Here's a little secret. That company now pays me every month to advertise their business on my talk shows.

Let's go back to the beginning and show you all the crap I've shoveled in my twenty years as an entrepreneur. From slinging cell phones, to opening retail stores selling motorcycle gear, to writing and producing music and playing at coffee shops for fifteen dollars per night, I have done it all.

Notes

Humble Beginnings

If you have read any of my other books, then you probably know my story. I was a kid that grew up in a broken home, was physically abused and a troubled youth with bad grades. I was born in Lakenheath, England to parents both in the Air Force. We came to the states when I was only one. Maybe ten years ago, I was given a file from my childhood and in it were hospital records and it was there I discovered the issues my parent had started before I was even born. They fought a lot. I remember being a toddler and the toaster flying across the room. When I was five, my mother left. I was to be raised by my father with an iron fist.

Having such a difficult childhood, I could have made excuses for myself, but I didn't. I worked hard, held myself accountable and made something of myself. When I was in school, I was a terrible student. I think a lot of it was boredom. I hated history, but today I collect American History artifacts. I spend a lot of my time reading and learning about America's past and why things are the way they are. So why wasn't I interested in school? I never went to college. Neither did my parents, nor my brother or sister.

I started my first official business at the age of seventeen. Around age fifteen, I started writing music and making cassettes to sell to the kids at school. I remember going to the thrift store and buying books on cassette, then using nail polish remover and erasing the words on the face of the cassettes. I would then apply a piece of tape over the holes at the top and record my music one by one onto each of the cassette. I would then draw the artwork for each cassette by hand and sign each one. If one of the cassettes didn't sell at school, I would put them on consignment at the local music store. I would call each week asking if any of my cassettes sold and for month, not one sold. After about a year, I called one week and was pleasantly surprised that I had five bucks waiting for me at the store.

A couple years would pass, and I felt it was time for me to actually build a real business. I wanted to get rich and I wanted fast money. Little did I know that fast money usually turns into fast failure. I had no idea where to start. One day, I started by buying and selling cellular phones on eBay. I would purchase used Nokia cellular phones, refurbish them and sell them online and in various places. After about a year, I found myself in a little bit of trouble and was forced to close the business. I knew what I was trying to do but didn't have the skills or discipline to execute it properly. Essentially, I was just another small business statistic, failing after only a couple years in business and leaving behind a ton of debt and bad credit.

It was at that point, I really needed to focus on my music career. That was where my heart was anyway. I started performing as many shows as I could and was constantly writing and releasing new music. Eventually I would find myself with a manager and making a living traveling playing music professionally. Though I was building in popularity around Northern California and Nevada, I wasn't making any real money and had to rethink where my life was taking me.

A few months would pass, and I met a gentleman carrying a bunch of motorcycle helmets into his apartment. I asked him the story with the helmets and asked how I could become a local dealer and with a little convincing, I started selling motorcycle helmets and accessories for the company. This is what propelled my potential as a business owner.

Though I was only twenty-six years old, I was starting to develop as an entrepreneur by trying new things and not being afraid to make mistakes. I would try one thing, then fail, then try something else. That would succeed and then I'd try something and fail again. Still playing shows several nights a week and selling helmets out of my apartment during the day, things started to make sense. My girlfriend came home from work one day and the house was filled to the ceiling with helmets. Literally hundreds of helmet boxes lined the walls of the apartment. This was when I started taking helmets out to the flea markets. The flea markets were a huge success prompting every motorcycle shop in town to start bringing their inventory out to get a piece of the action.

Eventually I would start opening retail stores. If I knew then what I know now about business, I would probably still own a bunch of successful motorcycle and racing shops.

Months turned into years and years into almost a decade and with the power of the recession of 2008, by 2012 it was all gone. Everything was gone. I took too many risks when I should have been buckling down and only experience will teach you that. I was now homeless and sleeping of a buddy's floor. I chose one day that sleeping in my car was better idea and then with the power of determination, I started my next business... Media.

Notes

Selling Cars

If you ever want to know what it takes to be a professional sales person, go get a job selling cars. These folks don't mess around. They will not let you waste their time and if you can't sell, you're gone. I would see sales people come in and before the ink was dry on the application, they were fired because they couldn't close the deal. Car dealerships are a little different today than they used to be, but they are just as ruthless. They used to be a group of sales guys standing in the sun calling colors. Basically, what that means is, as a car is pulling in, whoever calls the color of the car first gets to work the deal. Today however, technology rules the automotive business.

Today, car dealerships have their team of sales guys sitting at computers responding to leads that come off the internet and cold calling past clients. This presents an issue. Most experienced sales people aren't very computer savvy and most computer savvy sales people aren't really great sales people. A lot of them, if not most of them, cannot think on their feet. And this brings me to problem Number one… Scripts.

Most car dealerships today train their sales people to speak from a script. There's one major problem with this. They sound like a robot. You cannot train a person to handle rebuttals and real-life situations or become better sales people if they are memorizing the words to say. They will not understand what the customer actually needs. You cannot problem solve if you're speaking in a riddle. Years later I'll be sitting here and making my daily cold calls and remember something I was taught while selling cars and chuckle to myself because it doesn't and cannot apply to anything real life. People aren't stupid. They aren't going to buy a car from somebody who's phony. By teaching the proper steps to a sale and properly training sales people to become better, this is what will reflect in improved sales.

The next issue with the car business is not letting the sales people use their skills to make the business profitable. When I was selling cars, I already had ten plus years of sales under by belt, but they wanted me to learn scripts and stand on the point to call colors. As soon as the boss would turn around, I would be back on the phone calling dead deals. The other sales guys called it smiling and dialing. Let's just say I was a beast. I would ask my sales manager for all of the TD Deals, deals that were turned down for whatever reason. Whether it was a FICO issue, or down payment issue, or even time on the job, I didn't care. I wanted them in front of me to try again. A lot of times we got the deal done.

The sales people loved it. The dealership, not so much. Why? Because I found a way to work as little as possible and make a killing. Every weekend, the sales people would get spiffs for write ups. A spiff is like a little cash bonus for bringing somebody in and writing them up. Whether the car sold or not, the sales guy still got the spiff. I would call dead deal after dead deal and tell them that I was reviewing their file and may have found a way for them to get into a car, but they had to come down and see me. Most of them complied. Some just never showed back up for their appointment. The others just hung up on me. I would schedule as many appointments as I could. Some weekends, I would have half a dozen or more people coming in to see me. This resulted in a lot of spiffs and a lot of deals. Whether we sold the customer a car or not, I still got my fifty bucks for bringing the guy in. Six write-ups in a weekend equated to three-hundred dollars in spiffs before commissions. I usually sold at least a couple of deals in a weekend and the dealership would be happier than a mouse in a cheese factory when they handed out all that spiff money.

The other issue I ran into was letting management know all the mistakes they were making. I remember my boss calling me in when I sold Dodge and saying, "this is NOT Quinn Motors. You cannot run this business. You need to do what you're told." Then months later I was selling for Nissan, and a boss calls me in and says, "This is not Quinn Motors. You need to let US run the business.

Go sell something." The irony is when I started selling mortgages, and my boss called me in and said, "This is NOT Quinn Mortgage." As much as I'd love to say this didn't happen, it actually did. I realized at this point, it's going to be really tough for me to keep a job. The managers loved my numbers but hated how big of a pain in the ass I was.

On my days off from selling cars, I would have scheduled just as many clients to come in and see me, if not more, but would tell them that if I wasn't there, to see another sales person and they would help them out. This resulted in half deals every Monday morning when I came to work. How most dealerships justify who gets the deal is, whoever initiated the deal and whoever closed the deal shares the commission. If I initiate a deal and I give it to Joe and then he hands it off to Mike, Joe loses his commission because he turned himself out of the deal. Most sales guys in the car business work seven days a week and if not seven, definitely six. I would work five but was smarter about how I did it. The irony was, I was rebuilding my business and was still selling racing parts on the side and building my company you all know today. So, when I wasn't working a deal, I was on my phone working a different kind of deal. My boss would complain that I was always on the phone but couldn't say anything because my numbers were better than the rest of the other sales guys.

My father always told me to use my head and not my back. I knew what to say, without a script and did my job and made more money there than most of the other sales people. There were days I would make more than a grand in one day. Some days I'd make a grand and I did it by not even being at work, because I knew the power of cold calling and setting good appointments.

Notes

The Pursuit

There is a movie that I think every entrepreneur needs to see at least once. It stars Wil Smith playing the role of Chris Gardner, a down on his luck entrepreneur that gets an opportunity of a lifetime to give his son the life he deserves. He had to sacrifice a lot and by jumping in with both feet and putting everything on the line. He eventually became a multi-millionaire. A lot of you reading this are probably thinking it's easier said than done, but it's not as hard as you think. It really comes down to your state of mind and your willingness to do whatever it takes to follow your heart. Success is all mentality. Where is your head? Who do you want to be? Where do you want to be? And when?

The Pursuit of Happyness has one point where Chris Gardner is talking about the value of time and efficiency when making his cold calls and then gets into his strategy which is what made him more successful than the rest of the other candidates in the internship program. He references the use of

X=X=X=X, then talks about how he worked the list backward rather than forward. This was a very important lesson and can be used by every single one of us, every single day. By working the list backward, he was not only able to get to the higher profile clients quicker, everybody else was working the beginning of the list, bombarding the weaker clients several calls selling the same thing. What happens when telemarketers are calling over and over? You quit answering. So, when the competition was calling all of the same people over and over, they were getting little if no response from those leads, giving all of the meat on the bone to Chris.

By thinking different, he set himself apart from rest of the room. This is what you need to do when building your call lists. Where are you getting your lists? Are you paying for leads? How valuable are those leads? We're going to get into this more in a little bit.

Notes

Finding Leads

When you're building your business, the most important form of marketing is word of mouth. Do you agree? If not, then you really need to listen up. Your friends, family and past clients will literally make or break your business. If you are not getting repeat business and the community isn't talking about your product, then how do you plan on surviving?

Imagine if every single one of your clients gave you a referral every single time they did business with you. What would that do for your business? You would probably do pretty well. Don't you think? Not only do I think so, I know so. Now think about those referral clients now coming in to see you and now giving you their referrals. What would that do for your business then? It sounds pretty awesome doesn't it? That is what I am going to challenge you to do.

Regardless of the business you're in, whether it's car sales or dentistry, I want you to try this! Call five of your best clients and ask them for a stack of business cards of their clients or contacts. Make sure they know they will never see those business cards again. Most business people have about a hundred business cards in a drawer of people they frequently use or have run into a long the way. A lot of business owners even have stacks of junk cards by people they have never done business with. Those are great too. In return you will give them about the same amount of business cards from your contact list. Now, I want you to catalogue all of those names, email addresses, and phone numbers in an Excel Spreadsheet. I will explain how I want this done later. In the meantime, keep reading.

Next, I want you to call the next top client of yours and do it again. I want you to do this consistently adding new people to your list every single week. You will find yourself with thousands of names, email addresses and phone numbers in your database in no time at all. Make sure of two things.

1) Make sure when you list the name in excel, you include who referred the client.

2) Make sure you're moving the cards along to your next client. Client one's cards now go to client two. Client two's cards now go to client three and so on.

Notes

Your Contacts

It is very important that you use your list exactly like I recommend. I have used this formula for over a decade and have made millions of dollars using only Microsoft Excel and my cell phone. When you start using the formula for yourself, you will see how easy and efficient it really is.

Step 1: Create a New Spreadsheet.

Step 2: Understand the Columns.

Column A: Client's Name
Column B: Type of Business
Column C: Phone Number
Column D: Email Address
Column E: 1st Attempt Contact (leave blank)
Column F: 2nd Attempt Contact (leave blank)
Column G: 3rd Attempt Contact (leave blank)
Column H: Name of source of Referral

Step 3: Understanding the Color Chart

    White: Lead not yet touched
    Yellow: Attempted Contact, No Contact
    Orange: Contact Made / Follow Up
    Burgundy: Not Interested or MIA
    Red: DNC or Do Not Contact
    Blue: Sold Deal but Not Closed
    Green: Closed and Paid

Step 4: Understanding Pages

You'll see Sheet 1, Sheet 2, Sheet 3 at the bottom of your spreadsheet. I want you to change those to A, B, C, D, E, etc. All the way to Z. On each of these pages, you will put the lead's first name accordingly on those pages. This allows for easy organization and quick reference. You want to be able to click A and see every client with the first name starting with letter A. You will also be able to see how many Yellow, Orange and Blue deals are available and need to be contacted. You do NOT need to type in notes on any of these files. You should be able to determine the status of every lead quickly by understand what color is being used.

When you're looking at a page of leads and you see Yellow, you'll know immediately that you have not spoken to this person and there may be a deal there. Call them and try moving the deal forward. When you see an Orange lead, you'll know that you have made contact with that person and there may be some interest there. Call them and try moving the deal forward. When you see a Blue lead, you'll know it's a sold deal but are waiting on payment. Call them and get an ETA for payment. Your goal is to get every deal either Red for DNC or Green for CLOSED.

Notes

Getting Started

Now that you have input your leads into the spreadsheet, it's now time to understand HOW to execute the Cold Call Process. There are two ways to make cold calls. The right way, where you get results and people want to do business with you. Or, the wrong way when people hang up on you and block your number. I can honestly say that when I make my cold calls today, maybe one person per month will actually hang up on me and that is simply because I am non-intrusive, and I follow the system precisely to ensure that I get the results I expect. I am polite and not pushy but am always on high alert looking for an opportunity to close a deal.

Before you make ANY calls, you need to attempt contact another way first. That first initial contact should ALWAYS be by email. If you cannot find their email address, most often times if you take that person's name and phone number and punch them into Google and type email address, you will find it. The email you send should be a form email that goes to every single person consistently. I like to send an email maybe one a week to all of my thousands of contacts. Most often times, it will end up in a junk folder, but that is okay. The point is to make contact and have an "in" when you call them. Now, after you have sent that FIRST email, make sure you update Column E with today's date and mark it Yellow. Two things happened. You attempted contact with the email and Yellow means a contact attempt was made.

A lot of companies use Salesforce or other CRM systems to conduct daily business. They say it's efficient. There's one issue with these formats. Most companies want notes taken after each attempted call or after a phone conversation explaining what happened on that call. Here's the way I see it. WHO CARES WHAT HAPPENED? THEY DIDN'T BUY ANYTHING. So, why put notes at all? By simply marketing it Yellow tells you that you've attempted contact and got nowhere. That means to try again later.

I would recommend calling leads two to three days apart. Don't hound people but make yourself present. Don't be afraid to hop on Facebook and add them as a friend as well. They may already be friends with you and know all about what you do but are just too busy to answer or don't recognize your phone number. Regardless, unless they say never to call again, there's probably a deal there.

Notes

Making Calls

You're going to have to trust me on this and follow my directions precisely. I guarantee that you will get into your own head and let your ego dictate what happens here, but that is only going to make yourself inefficient, effecting how the system works and how many calls you make. You want results, right? Then do it exactly like this!

Now that it's time to start making calls, you need get your phone out and set it in front of you and preferably on speaker phone. You are going to make four calls per minute using this system. If they answer, keep the call to under one minute unless there are buying signs. We will get into those later. The point here is to reach as many people as possible in one sitting. I can make three hundred calls in an afternoon or as many as five hundred in about six hours of calling, closing several deals and talking to as many as twenty-five or more people.

Make sure that when you're making calls, your spreadsheet is right in front of you and ready and DO NOT GET BORED. Have excitement in your voice and make sure you follow my lead-in.

Step 1: Dial the number
Step 2: Put it on speaker phone
Step 3: Only let the phone ring for 15 seconds
Step 4: If no answer after 15 seconds, hang up
Step 5: Mark today's date in Column F
Step 6: Immediately dial the next

Two things will happen, either they answer, or they don't. DO NOT leave a voice message. Ever. Why? For one, you're burning valuable energy speaking when you don't need to be. Two, they will never call back a sales person. Three, you're wasting time when you could be making more calls. Four, if they see a missed call, chances are they will call back giving you an opportunity to close them.

If they do answer, your conversation should remain under one minute UNLESS they are genuinely interested. Buying signs are important to identify. If they start asking questions about the product and start placing themselves in the situation, chances are they are interested. Don't be afraid to ask them about their current product and whether it's working out for them or not. This gives you an opportunity to find a solution to a problem and make the deal.

When they answer, use this "script". Please make it your own, but make sure you say it exactly the same way every single time. Here's the one I use.

"Hello Joe? (wait for them to respond). Hey,

this is Quinn from The Good Life Show on 105.5. I just wanted to circle back around and see if you had a chance to review the information I sent regarding showcasing your business on our show."

Two things will happen, either they saw the information, or they didn't. We are referring to the email we sent them days prior.

If they saw it, ask them if it looks like something they would be interested in. Do not be pushy. These people do not know who you are. Most times, they will not have seen the email. Here is your follow up.

"Ok, here's what I will do. I am going to send you a quick text message with the information and a link to our website. Please take a moment to review it and see if it looks like it'll be a good fit. I will circle back around next week. Does that work for you?"

Two things will happen here. If they say, "Sure", it usually means they are taking even a little interest. Mark it Orange and follow up in a few days. If they say "No", it means they're not interested. Simply mark the file Burgundy and type Not Interested in Column F.

Now, if you made contact and they show a little interest, send them the text message as promised and mark the file Orange. Circle back around in a few days or week. Do not bombard these contacts, however stay on them. I have more people tell me it's impressive at how persistent I am and eventually do business with me, than tell me to never call again and hang up on me. If you're non-intrusive, you will get business from these people sooner or later.

Even if you mark a file Not Interested, you will still be contacting them again in a few months. I love seeing Not Interested leads turning into Closed deals. It happens all the time. Just be patient.

After you have:

1) Sent the email in Column E
2) Made the initial call in Column F
3) Attempted again in Column G
4) And still no answer by attempt 4...

I want you to mark the lead Burgundy and move on. When you get to the end of your list from A all the way through Z and everything is marked either, Red for DNC, Burgundy for Not Interested/No Contact or Green for Closed, mark ALL of the No Contact leads Yellow and work them again. There are deals there. You just have to find them. What you will find is that people that you have tried calling before that never answered their phone are now answering giving you an opportunity to make the deal happen. Maybe they have been getting all of your emails and haven't needed your product until now. Don't be afraid to text some of these people if you're not getting anywhere with them. If I get to the end of a lead with 4 attempts and never made contact, I will send a quick text with who we are and what we do with a link. There are times when I get an, "I'm Interested". Immediately, I pick up the phone and call them and now we have a deal.

Now, what does Blue and Green mean? Earlier, I said Blue was SOLD and Green in CLOSED. Aren't those the same thing? The answer is NO. How many times have you had a client interested and once you sent the invoice to be paid, they just disappear and never pay the invoice? It happens very very often, especially the business I'm in. So, BLUE means that they are interested, and we have sent out the invoice but are waiting for payment.

Here is a very important lesson for you. DO NOT CHASE PEOPLE DOWN. If they are going to pay you, they will. If they don't, move on. So, in order to handle this, when somebody becomes interested, mark the lead BLUE and in Column E, put today's day and let them know that payment needs paid in however many days you're willing to wait. I tell my clients seventy-two hours. I will make three attempts to follow up regarding collecting payment. A few days after I send the invoice to the client, I will reach back out again and put that date in Column F, then again, a few days later in Column G. And if no payment a couple of days after that, I mark it Not Interested, color it Burgundy and move on to the next lead. A client that is a pain in the ass before getting paid will be an even bigger pain in the ass after getting paid. We're in the business to make money, not babysit adults.

What happens after payment comes in? Mark it GREEN and move onto the next client. Congrats, you've made money and after providing services, ask them for business cards to add to your list and keep moving the leads forward. Make sure to follow up with your clients periodically. Make sure you're providing them value and quality. Don't be afraid to ask them for reviews. By simply following up with them, this opens new conversation for future repeat business. Usually when you work with somebody more than once, the deals get bigger and bigger because trust is built, and you have followed through with quality and service.

Notes

Referrals

Earlier in this book I mentioned Column H containing the name of the person who had supplied the lead's name. Make sure you are giving back to your clients who are helping you succeed. This column is a very important tool and serves two purposes. I make sure to give my clients who refer business to me twenty percent back in credit to be used toward more of my company's services. If the person they referred spends a thousand dollars with me for instance, that client who referred them to me now has a two hundred dollars in credit for more services which comes in hand around renewal time.

The second reason for having their name in Column H is for when the prospect you're talking to asks where you heard about them. Having that name handy makes the whole conversation shift into friendly banter. Once that conversation shifts to a friendly one, you can now talk about your relationship with that person and get to know their relationship. After the call, they usually go back to the person who referred them and helps that client move toward doing business with your company. This is the proper use of word of mouth advertising. You have a community around you. Use it.

I think where people get work of mouth advertising wrong is when they WAIT for people to talk about your business. Unfortunately, you cannot wait for ANYTHING in business. YOU have to be moving forward and creating innovative ways to reach new people. Look around you. There are hundreds, if not thousands of like business in your community. Who are the people doing well and what are they doing different? If you continue to do the same thing as everybody else, how do you expect your business to stand out from the rest? If the majority of like businesses in your community are just getting by and you're doing the same marketing and have a comparable product, how could you expect your business to be any better than the competition? You can't, and you won't and if the market shifts in any way, the weaker businesses will be swept away by the stronger ones.

Notes

Rebuttals

With making sales calls every day, there is a one hundred percent change somebody will not want what you're trying to sell. There is nothing wrong with somebody telling you they aren't interested or that your price is too high. What is wrong however, is how you handle those rebuttals and how you bring that potential client closer to a sale.

There are pushy rebuttals that will kill your deal or any chance of a deal and then there are the rebuttals that answer the questions and remove doubt. What are they and how do they work? The last thing you want to do is piss somebody off who is just asking qualifying questions to see whether or not you can provide them with value. Believe me, I have pissed plenty of people off and killed more than enough deals.

The most common "excuse" I get is "I'm not interested". When I was selling cars, hanging up after a client said they weren't interested was a major no-no and sometimes an offense that would get you fired. Before we get into the meanings of "excuses", let's get into identifying what the excuses actually mean.

When dealing with the public every day, I see most people making a major mistake in HOW they listen to words people say. It's like that person that talks behind your back and spells out your every flaw. It's not they hate you, but rather they envy you and their insecurities are fueling their trash talk. You'll never hear an ugly person say that another person is ugly. It's always the pretty person but the pretty person feels ugly inside and them saying the other person is ugly makes themselves feel better. Does that make sense? So instead of listening to their words of how ugly that person is, listen to the story of why that person is saying what they are saying.

Here's another example:

Mary had a little lamb. What does this mean? Does she have the lamb, or does she no longer have the lamb? If you listen to the words, it says she no longer has a lamb. However, if you listen to the story you'll know she still has the lamb. You need to apply this thinking into every single transaction you encounter. Apply this to your daily life as well too. You'll find yourself reading people better than the guy next to you and this always giving you the advantage.

When I check in to a hotel, I always ask for a discount, but I never actually ask for the discount. I use a story rather than words and that creates action. I walk in to the hotel and check-in and the host tells me the room is two hundred dollars per night plus twenty-five dollars per day for parking. I'll respond with, "Oh sheesh. I didn't know I was paying for parking tonight too. Sigh. Are there any programs or incentives I could apply for that would wave that by chance?" Often times, they will just wave the fee and with a smile and eye contact, thank them. I never actually "asked" for a discount, but I got it exactly what I wanted. Now, let's apply this to cold calls.

What does "not interested" actually mean? Either they are busy and want to get off the phone with you or they are really, just not interested. So, when they say they aren't interested, a simple rebuttal of, "let me ask you something, did you have a chance to see the information we sent over to you?" They will either respond with a yes or no. If they say yes, then respond with, "So you read about what we can provide you and you just don't see any value in what we can provide you?" This will open up the conversation. If you aren't getting anywhere with the transaction in a reasonable amount of time, mark the date on Column on E, F, or G and move on to the next lead. If they respond with no, they haven't seen your information, then send the text message and tell them you will follow up in a few days.

One of the things I have learned after two decades of sales is, these people are adults. You shouldn't have to strong arm anybody to buy your product. Keep them in your database and keep calling them according to this system. Eventually, they will buy from you or tell you to remove them from your list. This brings me to an important point. If somebody says anything like, "remove me from your list" or, "don't call me anymore", you are required by law to remove them and refrain from ever contacting that person again, UNLESS they opt back in for contact.

Here's the next excuse. I get this one all the time and there are a few ways to make this one work. "I can't afford it."

This is not as common for smaller purchases but very common with new car purchases. I get this one all the time selling advertising for small businesses. This is also very easy to overcome if, done properly. "I can't afford." "Let me ask you… What if I could not make it fit into your budget, but actually save you money each month?" Now you are piquing their interest and finding a solution to a problem. Again, you were non-intrusive and not pushy. When I hear this excuse when calling small businesses to sell advertising on my talk shows, I always ask, "What if I broke it up into payments over twelve months?"

Let's say a customer is looking at a year's worth of advertising and the total is two thousand, four hundred dollars. A lot of small businesses don't have that kind of money laying around, especially for advertising. They know that they need the product for their business but spending a lump sum like that hinders the reserves for that business. By offering the same product for two hundred dollars per month, we close the deal, improve their business and six months down the road when business has picked up, we can offer them more of our products. But, had we not found a solution, we would get nothing. Not a deal, nor the relationship and the referrals that business sends our way.

Sales is nothing more than providing a solution to a problem. All we need to do is find out WHAT that problem is, and we have earned the customer's business. Years ago, I created an acronym for SALES.

Simple
And
Less
Expensive
Solutions

A sale must be **easy** for the customer. A sale must provide the customer **value**. And, a sale must provide a **solution** to a problem.

Have you heard of the 3P's or 3M's in a Sale?

Person, Price, Product or Man, Money, Machine.

Both are the same thing and apply to every single transaction the same way. The customer must LIKE YOU, THE PRICE, and/or THE PRODUCT. If they don't like TWO of any of those things, you have NO DEAL.

However, the price could be right for the customer and product could be exactly what they are looking for, but if they don't like you, you have NO DEAL. So, when you're making your cold calls, if you're pushy and you cannot quickly identify their problem and provide a solution to that problem, chances are you won't get the deal.

Notes

Understanding Marketing

The formula for marketing is very simple when you dumb it down. If you follow this very simple formula for your small business, you'll do very well. It's when you start getting into analytics and trying to use a big business' formula that you start wasting time and making yourself less efficient, which in turn, costs you money.

Frequency and Reach.

What does this mean? Marketing is nothing more than frequency and reach. How many people can you reach? How many times can you reach them and how many different ways can you reach them?

If you slowly start adding your leads in your spreadsheet as friends on Facebook, Instagram and Twitter, they will start seeing your posts. They will see your friend's posts. They also see your friend's of friends posts. Then, when they see your emails and even your text messages, you're starting to now make a positive impression. And then when you call, these people are already becoming familiar with what you do, and will either be interested or not interested what you provide. The community turns on the radio, there you are. They see your advertising on Google and other various websites. They see your posts on Facebook, Instagram and Twitter and start liking or even sharing your posts. Then what happens when you're speaking at an event or presenting before a group of people? Now you have credibility to go with it. Then one day, you're in public at a restaurant or supermarket and they walk up and introduce themselves and say hello, what is going to happen when they need you or your product or services? Who will they call? You. Why? Because you made yourself available to them and you stood out from your competition. If you keep doing the same thing as everybody else, how will set yourself apart?

Here's my next piece of advice. Whoever you are and what you've done, nobody cares. It sounds harsh but the reality of it is, all they care about is what you can do for them. If you cannot provide them with value, all of your awards and credentials don't mean anything. Make sure you can provide value, or you've got nothing.

Where do you start with your marketing? Large companies have millions and millions of dollars set aside just for marketing their business or product. This turns into future revenues to be budgeted for future marketing to create their business' cycle. With a small business, you don't have the millions of dollars sitting around to advertise your business, but in today's world, small businesses DO have the advantage. More people than ever want to work with small and locally owned businesses. They want to keep the money local and word of mouth advertising is what does this. You start with trading business cards like I mentioned before. Then work on your social media presence. Then look for local media forms like radio, tv, and magazines. Make sure to find cost effective mediums and don't be afraid to get creative. Get to know your local radio hosts. Talk to them about using your products and endorsing you in trade. The same goes for television personalities, magazine editors or even newspapers columnists. I hear people all the time say that the newspaper is dead. If that's the case, why is it still profitable? Because newspapers are online now and, on our devices, connected to social media. There is still a huge audience for print however, most news is delivered digitally today.

Notes

Repeating the System

It will take some considerable time to get through all of your leads, especially if you continue to grow your list. But, what happens when everything is marked, GREEN for Closed, Burgundy for No Contact or Not Interested, or RED for Do Not Call? The answer is simple. Mark all of the leads YELLOW, that you never got a hold of or the deal went nowhere. Start at letter A and start working the list again. You will now find that a lot of people know who you are may want to proceed.

Here's another issue you may run into. What happens if you're talking to a potential customer and they ask to follow up in six months? In Column E, type "Call July 6th" or whatever date you two agree on, mark it ORANGE and follow back up on that date. There is nothing wrong with keeping tabs on your potential deals. Please don't make the mistake of needing a ton of notes in your system. Notes mean nothing if they aren't buying anything.

What about if you're just not that good at sales? What if you're a beginner? What if you have never made cold calls before and you're afraid of rejection?" These are all questions I get all the time. If you're afraid of being hung up on, then get hung up on. Dust yourself off and do it again. It's no different that asking a pretty girl or cute guy out. If they say no, you'll probably try a different way another time and hope for a yes. Eventually, somebody else will come around and you'll get your shot. And then when that happens, you'll feel like stud and go for another one. It's not rocket science. You just need to be patient and persistent.

What happens after the deal is made? I personally like to follow up with my clients consistently and see how well I am doing. Sometimes, I get news I don't want to hear, and they tell me that I let them down. This is where I can try to make it up to them, provide more value and possibly even make another deal with the client which is great for business. Just make sure that you're true to yourself and you're providing quality and value.

Notes

The Entrepreneur's Why

Every single day, I speak with countless business owners and entrepreneurs. Some are from our geographical location and others from other parts of the globe. Nonetheless, they all share something in common... Passion. When I see a small business owner struggling day in and day out but continue to fight the good fight, as they say, it really makes to me think about their why. What drives them? Why do they choose to struggle with this idea of creating the dream by working for themselves instead of getting up every morning and going to a job?

I remember years ago, before I was a talk show host, before I was producing music professionally, before I was opening online stores, I was trying to build a name for myself. Somebody once told me that I could work to make somebody else rich or I could work to make myself rich. The decades that followed, I thought the word RICH was a term used for money. Then one day I was driven to read the book, Rich Dad Poor Dad by Robert Kiyosaki.

Robert spoke about the word RICH as a definition of lifestyle and the word WEALTH as the definition of the accumulation of money. I think what drives people, young entrepreneurs, small business owners and the like is the want or need to be rich. Some chase the money or shiny object as a local business coach told me, before she proceeded to call me arrogant and judgmental. It was the realization for me that the shiny object was not what would make us rich but the quality of life that Rich Dad speaks about that makes us get up each morning to struggle and challenge ourselves to be better.

I remember when I was in summer school between eighth and ninth grade and I was thinking about life after high school. I saw all my friends' parent struggling to make ends meet. I saw my own parents barely making enough to pay the bills. They would leave for work early every morning, giving me enough time to bring my friends over to play video games before school, if we even went at all. They were too busy to know either way. And then would come home every night after dark, too late to find out if we ever did our homework or not. That summer sitting there in class, I started doing the math, comparing either to get a job with the little education I'm receiving, or start a business and make as much money as I want. I remember thinking of ways I could start a skateboard retail business selling the kids at school skateboard parts at a profit. Those days of thinking are the same things entrepreneurs in their thirties, forties, fifties or older think about every single day. They are looking for a better way.

This is the passion I am talking about. These people absolutely love what they do. Both for their community as well as for their family. They slave over their business each and every day, making a name for themselves and hoping they make enough money to bring home to their families giving their children the life they never had. It's the American way. It's the principles our nation was founded on and it's why it is most important to support our local small business community and give back as much as we can.

If you're thinking about starting a small business or are one of millions of entrepreneurs in our country trying to make ends meet, I want you to ask yourself a question. Are you doing what you love to do? Are you passionate about your business? Or, are you in business because the money is good? I can honestly say that in my business, I would build talk shows, produce music and write books regardless of whether it made money or not, because for the first twenty years, it barely made any. By following my dream and striving to be better every single day and by providing value to my clients, it has given me the life I have always dreamt of.

Notes

Training Your Sales People

I see too many sales organizations today pushing for more sales people rather than making their current sales people better. It is very expensive for a sales organization to hire new sales people to bring better results and then firing the weaker sales people only after a month or so of poor production. This is honestly like throwing your old TV away because there is nothing to watch.

I remember years ago when I first got into sales. My first sales job was at Samsonite in Vacaville, California. I was seventeen. I would ride my bike nine miles each way back and forth to work. If it rained, I would wear a waterproof suit with my slacks, button-down shirt and tie underneath. After a long shift, I would typically change into my other work clothes and head on over to my graveyard shift security job at an auto parts distribution facility. I wasn't very good at sales, but I was a hard worker and my boss admired that. I showed up on time, did the best I could do and went home. After a few months, I found it wasn't for me and quit.

Shortly after this stint, I realized I was ready to officially start my first business. Again, I wasn't very good at sales, but I was a fast talker, a thinker and was innovative. After about a year in business, I found myself in a little bit of trouble and shut it down. I was now 19. A couple years would pass, and I'd get a job at a car dealership selling cars. I only lasted about month here before I was let go. Why am I telling you this? My sales managers admired my hard work, but they never sat me down and taught me HOW to properly talk to people. All they taught me were shady sales tactics and scripts. This is how most sales organizations are run these days.

There are plenty of sales training classes and seminars out there and from what I have found, these courses are teaching sales people to memorize scripts. This is NOT how you train sales people. Sales really is just thinking on your feet and being great at your craft of problem solving. You cannot teach people a script to solve common problems on the sales floor. In addition, poor sales performance comes from lack of interest or just being crapped out. I believe that most sales people are really good at their craft but the organization itself is what is harming the sales and performance of the sales people. Poor pay, poor marketing and the organization not having the right focus in mind spins the sales person's mind, impairing their ability to sell.

Sales organizations put fear in sales people and with sales being a mental-based business, the sales person gets in their own head and literally paralyzes their ability to close the deal. Unfortunately, most sales organizations today lack in the uplifting and positive environments and are most focused on their bottom end resulting in cut backs. I went back and sold cars again in 2013. I had just shut down my second business and was pretty much homeless. I took too many calculated risks with my retail stores during the recession and couldn't pull out of it, like most entrepreneurs in that time.

I pull up to Sacramento Dodge in my Porsche with my laundry basket in the bonnet. I sit down with the sales manager and explain to him the situation. He asks where I live. I look over at my car. At this time, I am 30 years old, in a suit, my old beat up Porsche parked outside and looking for a sales job. I had already made my first million with my previous business, but like most people after the recession, I was broke. They hire me on the spot. Within a couple of weeks, I am at the top of leaderboard. A couple months would pass, and I am spun out like the rest of the sales people complaining that the leads are weak, like from the movie Glengarry Glen Ross. The leads weren't weak, I was weak, and the organization was breaking us. A few months later, the dealership was bought out by another company and everybody went separate ways.

At this point, I found myself working at Paramount Equity Mortgage. Say what you want, this was a wonderful and eye-opening experience for me. I feel like this organization made me the sales professional I am today. Without these hard-working people, I wouldn't have had the training and support I needed to become successful. I will say however that as their sales expectations grew within the company, so did the stress and our quality of life. Why was this? It was simply because they were hiring more and more sales people and had to cut corners in the training of the staff, affecting the quality of the employees brought on board. Yes, the company made more money, but also resulted in many class-action lawsuits costing the company millions of dollars long after those employees found employment elsewhere. It's not uncommon for me, years later, to open the mailbox and get another $500.00 check from a class-action lawsuit.

Another huge mistake management takes today is overworking their sales people. I see sales people working ten, twelve or more hours each day to hit their quotas. This may seem productive because they are working more hours, but the mental fatigue ultimately is making a lot of those hours useless also causing them to resent their jobs. Management can properly train and encourage their sales teams to get the results they would expect, allowing the sales people to work less hours, enjoy their jobs, spend time with their families and giving the organization less turnover.

So, my advice is this. If you're starting or currently running a sales organization, you need to sit and speak with your employees, have empathy and find out HOW you can better their lives. People are NOT motivated by money. They are motivated by family and what that money can do. So, instead of spiffs and one hundred-dollar bonuses, maybe a day off and dinner out on the town with their spouse is a better approach. They come back to work refreshed and ready for another productive day.

Notes

Expect Good Things

The saying goes you must give to receive. You must give respect to get respect. You must give love to get love. And you must give money if you want something in return. The same goes for your business. If you don't give your business one hundred percent, it won't give it back. My advice to any business owner is to love your business like a child. It's born, it lives, it thrives, and it even makes you proud. It puts a smile on your face. It makes you cry. It's a breathing, living, growing extension of you and someday, like everything in this world, it will die. But, like everything you do, if you love it, cherish it, raise it to be successful, it will love you back.

I remember when I was building my first business. It wasn't really a business at all but more so, was a part of me. I am referring to my music. From day one, I always thought ahead. I knew right out the gate marketing my brand as my real name would be almost impossible, considering my biological name is Robert Jones. I knew I needed to create something catchy. I needed to create something unique and it had to be timeless. I used names like

John Michael Montgomery, a country singer in the 1990s and David Lee Roth, a rock singer from the 1980s as a reference. I came up with Jon Robert Quinn. I was 17 years old at the time. I took Jon from Jones, Robert, my first name and Quinn, my mother's maiden name creating the brand that everybody knows today. This was just like naming a child. I knew that this journey would be a long one and I was in it to win it.

Throughout the years, I have owned retail stores, written several books, produced a ton of music, built talk shows, appeared on television, even did a little acting, and everything has been under the name Jon Robert Quinn. Why is this? There are two reasons really. One is because I am passionate about my business and the second reason is because rebranding yourself takes a lot of time and energy and getting that message to the community is very expensive.

I think one of the most expensive things in life is education. I am not talking about a college education, though that is very expensive as well, but more so talking about the lessons we learn in life. We make mistakes and that sometimes costs us a lot of money, relationships, even marriages. Your business has the same trials as life. I think one of the biggest mistakes people make with their business is not taking it serious enough. A lot of people are afraid to take that leap of faith and go all in. They have one foot in and one foot out. A lot of times they have a part-time or even full-time job as well. A lot of times I will tell an entrepreneur to quit their job and climb into the trenches. Getting into survival mode and not being able to make rent or even eat builds character and makes us THINK. Without thinking, we cannot succeed.

I work with a lot of local businesses hosting business talk shows in the region. I currently host 9 shows in Sacramento alone and currently work with over 200 local businesses. I see a lot of what business owners go through. I see the mistakes they make. I know who's making money and who isn't. I even know who thinks they are making money but will most likely be out of business in the next couple of years because they don't have the proper foundation set for their business. Too many people are trying to perfect the hamburger without getting the product out to the community and building a following. One business I am very impressed with is a company called Detoxination Wellness Centers. These guys have a unique product and are not only innovative but are using science to give people an all-natural approach to become healthier.

What I find most appealing about working with these people is the fact that dad created this system, implemented it, built it into a sustainable model and the son now is taking the company to the next level. It doesn't stop there. These fine folks are creating helpful tools for people all over the world, creating new streams of income and reaching more people to help more people. This is loving your business like a child and creating a model that is sustainable for generations.

When your first child was born, what did you expect? You expected good things. You want your child to succeed. You want your child to fall in love. You want your child to someday make a child of their own, move out on their own and care for themselves. That is no different than a business. If the business is raised properly, it will outlive you. If raised properly, someday it will take care of you. If raised properly, it will branch out into other smaller businesses and someday grow into something as strong as its daddy. So, when starting your first business, love it like a child, give it everything it needs and expect good things.

Notes

In Conclusion

Why did you get into business? To make money. To do what you're passionate about. To build a legacy. Maybe you're just in sales and want to someday open a business. Like it or not, whether you're 1099 or a W2 wage earner, if you're in sales, you're in business for yourself. You need to look around you at what everybody else is doing and set yourself apart.

Before I let you go, I want to tell you one more story. When I was in the mortgage business, I was hungry. I was getting married soon and had just lost everything a year or so prior. I had to make something of myself, both for me, but also for my wife. I came in to work every day five minutes early. I would work through lunch eating at my desk and stay five minutes late every day. Why did I do this?

The answer wasn't so I could look busier than the rest of the sales team. It wasn't to show off to the bosses. It wasn't so I could make more calls in the off time. It was to prep. I came in every day early to see who was number one for the day and take a calculation of how many calls per hour the top person made, and my goal was to double that number. If I fell short, I was still number one. My first full month of making calls for the mortgage business, I complete seven hundred and fifteen transferred calls in a twenty-one-day month. Number two was over two hundred calls less than myself. I was immediately promoted.

I held myself accountable and made a game out of it. I had my date broken into hours and would strive to make more call in the second hour than the first and more in the third from the second. The point is, I was more efficient that the competition and that resulted in literally double the pay from the rest of the team because I closed more deals.

Use these tools I have given you. Follow this formula precisely and I guarantee you will be making more calls and closing more deals in no time at all. It's now time to make YOU The Cold Call King. Go kill it. Boom Baby!

Notes

Notes

Notes

Notes

Notes

Other Titles by Jon Robert Quinn

Books

- One Long Road: My Journey as a Musician & Recording Artist

- A Bigger Business with Better Results (2018)

- Being Quinnessential: Beginners Guide to Becoming a Gentleman (2018)

- Searching for Sara (2017)

- Tips to Increase Your Wealth, Health & Life (2009)

Music

- New Faces (2000)
- Solo-Fisticated (2004)
- One Long Road (2004)
- JeRQ THIS (2005)
- Live '05 (2005)
- JeRQ THIS TOO (2006)
- The Road to Hammerlane (2006)
- A New Beginning (2007)
- The Best of Jon Robert Quinn (2008)
- One Day at a Time (2009)
- JeRQ THIS 3 (2010)
- 1982 (2015)
- The Best of Jon Robert Quinn: Vol 2 (2016)
- Made in England (2017)
- Quinnessential: 20 Years (2018)

Talk Shows

- The Good Life Show with Jon Robert Quinn (2015)
- 60 Minute Success (2016)
- The Cash Cow Show (2017)
- Why Pay Six Percent Show (2017)
- Investor Profits Now (2017)
- Real Estate Investor Weekly (2017)
- Women's Wealth Warrior Show (2018)
- The Jon Robert Quinn Show (2018)
- The Everyday CFO (2018)
- The Body by Vlad Show (2018)
- License to Kill (2018)
- Your Perfect Home (2018)
- Get Detoxinated (2018)

www.ingramcontent.com/pod-product-compliance
Lightning Source LLC
Chambersburg PA
CBHW031537210526
45464CB00003B/1052